Helping you help yourself

Congratulations - you're about to change your life.

Not overnight. Not without a lot of work. But you **can** change and you **will** change, if you try out the suggestions here and keep putting them into practice.

Note we said 'try'. That's the point about this approach - you need to work at changing things. This way, you learn a lot about what makes you tick, and the changes you make tend to stick.

Because just reading isn't enough.

You'll benefit from working through the content again and again to apply it in your life.

Don't worry. You only have to do 15 things and one of them is grabbing a juice or putting the kettle on!

Are you ready for number 1?

THE TIME, THE PLACE, THE CHAIR, THE TEAPOT

Make a space to learn

You're wanting to change your life. What you're doing is very important and you must treat it that way.

Choose a time and place each day to read your little book. It's your space, your time for changing.

Make it a quiet, comfy place, but not too luxurious. Sitting at a table is better than lounging on the settee, for instance. You're working on your life – don't slouch.

Pour a juice or put the kettle on and make a cup of tea to drink while you're working. And make sure you have a pen and paper, or a phone/tablet to makes notes on.

Number 2

NO DISTRACTIONS, NO BISCUITS, NO IFS, NO BUTS

You need a clear focus when you're changing your life

Switch off notifications, or mute your phone.

Nibbling is also a distraction. If it's lunchtime, have lunch. Then go to your reading place and work on change.

TV is something else you don't need in the background, as is music. In fact, try to get rid of as much noise as possible.

Shut the windows if you're distracted by traffic noise. Close the door if people are passing by. Switch off the TV, the radio, the PC and your phone. If it's the time of day you might sometimes have some wine or a beer- skip it till you've done your work.

THE ENERGY THING

Steal a trick from the movies

Just before they go in front of the camera, a lot of actors run on the spot for a few moments, or press hard against the wall, or run up and down the stairs.

Our bodies link to our mental focus and motivation. So, doing this helps them get energised and adds an extra energy to their performance.

If you do the same before you sit down to work on change, you'll feel livelier and more able to do what it suggests. You'll also feel a bit more energetic and positive.

It doesn't really matter what you do, so long as it's something that uses your muscles.

You could do a few press-ups, touch your toes or jump up and down for a minute or two.

If your mobility isn't great, try pushing your hands together or stretching. Use these physical changes to energise you so you're ready for action.

Number
4

REPEAT IT 'TIL YOU KNOW IT BY HEART

If the book is falling apart, it probably means you aren't*

Don't just read the course resources- really work them into your life.

Read the content carefully and think about what it's saying. Ask yourself "How does this apply to me?" Make a note of words or ideas that help you better understand how you feel. Capture phrases or words that challenge or encourage you.

Learn in the way that suits you best. You might work through things in one longer session. Or do it in a series of shorter reading sessions. It doesn't matter which way you do it, just do it – again and again.

None of our resources have many words for a good reason – so that you can read them over and over until you know them off by heart.

So spend time reflecting on what you're learning and write it down in a learning diary - perhaps as a calendar entry or note on your phone. Set reminders there to prompt you to keep applying what you learn.

To do that you need something else ...

*Okay, if you're reading the book online or as an ebook, the pages won't fall out (not unless you drop your phone anyway.) But we hope you get the point.

DON'T JUST SIT THERE, MAKE A PLAN!

How to get what you're learning off the page and into your life

When you've read and re-read the content and really know it, it's time to make a plan. Decide what you're going to do or change and work out how you'll do it.

There is a Planner sheet on the next two pages that aims to help you make an effective plan. You don't need to fill it in now, you will have a chance to do that later.

You may find it helpful as you are reading through this book, to make a note of small, simple changes you would like to make. Number 6 will help you to do this.

All of the resources in this series include linked worksheets. They have spaces for you to gather information, or put what you are learning into practice. Writing things down is important- it helps us work out what we think, and aids our learning.

Remember, however you are using this- as a printed book, an e-book or online, you're working on changing your life and your regular sessions are about making plans and checking progress.

It's all about learning.

Planner Sheet

Make a Plan!

1. What am I going to do?

Just one small thing

2. When am I going to do it?

That way you'll know if you don't do it

3. What problems or difficulties could arise, and how can I overcome them?

4. Is my planned task -

	Yes	No
• Useful for understanding or changing how I am?	☐	☐
• Specific, so that I will know when I have done it?	☐	☐
• Realistic, practical and achievable?	☐	☐

My notes:

THINK ABOUT A CLIMBING WALL

You can do anything if you break it into bits

How do you get to the top of a climbing wall? In lots of small steps.

It's the same with making small, simple changes to your life. Even if your task looks enormous, you **will** be able to do it if you break it into bits.

Let's say you want to cut down social media use. You could break the week into bits and just stop on Mondays, for example.

If you want to get out more, just work on part of the problem - like leaving the house or walking round the park.

Or if you're spending too much, you could start by just cutting out online shopping.

Most tasks can be broken down like this, and you're much more likely to succeed when you do things bit by bit.

WHAT IF YOU GET STUCK?

Don't worry, everyone does

Everybody gets stuck or discouraged. Nobody can sail straight through an important change in life without feeling fed up or finding it difficult sometimes.

There are two things you can do to prepare for this:

1. Expect to get stuck from time to time. It's a sign that your human - not that you've failed.

2. Work out what to do about it in advance.

There are lots of things that can help you through the difficult patches.

Turn the page to find out more

ACCEPT THAT CHANGE IS LIKE A NEW YEAR RESOLUTION

And you know what happens to them

We're all the same at New Year. Lots of good intentions, lots of plans to change our lives.

But then, often just a couple of weeks into January, we slip and go back to the same old routines.

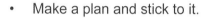

Here's what you do to stop your plan turning into a failed resolution:

- Make a plan and stick to it.

- Now, mark a **Review Day** on the same day every week for three months ahead. Why so long? Because you're working at setting up a new routine that sticks for the long-term.

- Use the **Review Sheet** on the next two pages to review the outcome of each plan.

Use the pattern of *Plan, Do* and *Review* to help you move forwards.

If you need more help, you could speak to a health worker such as your GP, or a trusted family member or friend to encourage you and check your progress.

You're doing well, keep reading!

living
life to
the full
www.llttf.com

Review Sheet

How did it go?   What did you plan to do?

Did you try to do it?   Yes ☐   No ☐

If yes: What went well?

What didn't go so well?

What have you learned from what happened?

How are you going to apply what you have learned?

If no: What stopped you?

You: (forgot, not enough time, put it off, didn't think I could do it, couldn't see the point etc.)

Other things: (other people, work or home issues, poor weather, transport difficulties etc.)

How can you tackle things differently next time?

Number **9**

GET YOUR FRIENDS, FAMILY AND CARERS ON THE TEAM

You don't have to do this alone

The more people you involve in your plan for change, the more likely it is to work out.

Right from the start, tell all the people you trust what you're doing and ask for their support. They'll be there for you when you struggle, or when doubts set in. Phone them up and tell them how you feel.

If you can, ask someone whose opinion you trust to help you to make changes. When you find things difficult, they will remind you why you're doing this and may even tell you things you don't want to hear.

That's what real friends are for.

Number
10

SIT DOWN AND WRITE YOURSELF A LETTER

Do it now, while you're all fired up

Imagine it's five years from now and you're sitting down to write a thank you letter to yourself.

Life has changed and moved on. You want to thank the person you were five years ago, for persevering, making the changes, sticking with things and keeping working on the future.

What would you write? Get your pen, turn the page and work it out.

Dear

I want to say thanks for sticking with
it five years ago

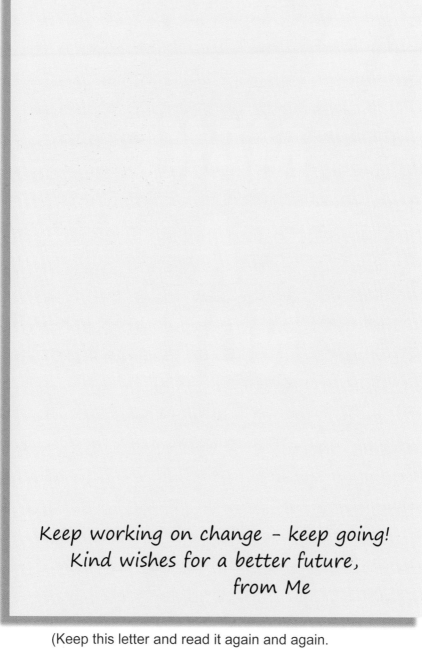

Keep working on change - keep going!
Kind wishes for a better future,
from Me

(Keep this letter and read it again and again.
It's your future. Don't throw it away).

Number
11

MAKE
A
NOTE

Remind yourself why you're doing all this

Pepper your fridge with post-it notes.

Write messages on them about why you want to change, what it will be like when you solve your problem, how great you're going to feel when it's done.

Now write some more and stick them in the bathroom, so you see them every morning.

Stick notes on the kitchen cupboards, on the TV, on the steering wheel if you have a car and on your desk, tool bag, locker or laptop. Arrange things so that your routine gets you face to face with at least ten messages each day. Plan encouraging reminders into your phone calendar as well so you receive reminders at times you know might be difficult.

And then, once a week, move them around so you don't get so used to seeing them you take no notice.

Number
12

GIVE YOURSELF SOME GOOD ADVICE

What would you say to your best friend?

Imagine it's not you with the problem, but your best friend. They were doing really well but have struggled recently.

What warm words of encouragement would you use to remind your friend that things will be better when the problem has improved? How would you gently encourage them to get back on track?

Now say all that to yourself. Give yourself the advice and support that you'd give to your very best friend. You deserve it.

THINK
LIKE
AN
ATHLETE

Get support wherever you can find it

Top athletes know they can't win alone. They look for a great coach and good advice and get help in every way they can.

You're just the same, so look around and get support from as many places as possible. It will help you stay on track and moving forward.

Accept help in any form that's useful - whether it's face to face from a practitioner or support worker, by telephone, by email, via a reading group, treatment group, friends or family, or from a voluntary sector worker or counsellor.

The more help you get, the more chance you have of making it.

MAKE
EVERY
SUPPORT
SESSION
COUNT

How to get the most out of formal counselling or psychological supports

To get the best from a supporter or practitioner you are talking to, don't clam up and say "um". Instead, work out what you want to talk about an hour or so beforehand.

Maybe you're feeling stuck. Do you want to discuss a different problem? Are you having trouble finding time to make the most of your book? Have you made good progress and want to know what's next?

The best time to think about these things is before your session, not in the middle of a meeting, email or phone/ video call.

UM...

BUILD YOUR MOTIVATION FOR CHANGE

You've got to have a reason

It's sometimes easy to either forget or talk yourself out of getting the support you need from practitioners or other support workers. So, if you're seeing a worker or practitioner, at the end of every session make sure you both know why it's worth your while to have that next contact.

Whether it's face to face, telephone, or online support, there's got to be a good enough reason to make you want to go back.
- Perhaps something you want to understand more?
- Or a new skill you need advice on?
- Or perhaps, you need someone to give you encouragement when you really need it?

That next appointment, follow up call or email could be the one that really helps make the difference to you and your life.

Use it, don't waste it.

Don't have a Supporter?
Turn to page 46.

Number
15

TURN UP
WITH
AN AGENDA

It will make your sessions really work

Even if you think about what you want to say beforehand, it's easy to forget when you're in the middle of a session.

Write about your progress and how you're feeling. Make a note of the things you're finding hard, and what may be getting in the way. Write down what's going well and make a list of the things you've learned.

Remember, the life you're changing is yours. The project is yours and the project manager is you. So get your pen and write the agenda for each of your sessions.

There is an example Agenda on the next page, and some suggestions on how to get the most out of the session on the page after.

Agenda

For discussion dated:

What's going well?

What's not going so well?

What have I learned from this?

How am I putting what I've learned into practice?

After the session, review what you learned

Getting the most out of the session

Download from

www.llttf.com/resources

Three key things I have learned:

1.

2.

3.

My Notes:

How can you remember what you have learned?

My Worksheets:

Putting what you have learned into practice.

My Plan*:

1. What am I going to do?

2. When am I going to do it?

3. What problems or difficulties could arise,
and how can I overcome them?

*Or use the Planner sheet.

HASSLE ME?

HASSLE ME?

HASSLE ME?

It's easy to miss support sessions

Perhaps something comes up? Maybe you're too busy and forget? Or decide you can't be bothered? Or maybe you're feeling good - great - and that next support appointment doesn't feel like it's needed? Or perhaps you've got a lot on and feel you don't have time for anything else, let alone a face to face session or phone call?

And so for times like these, it's useful to discuss in advance how much you want to be reminded, pestered or chased by your supporter.

A telephone call the next day, text or email might be helpful - or it could put you right off! You know what you're like, so talk about it and agree what would work best for you.

JUST ONE MORE THING

Now it's time to put what you've learned into practice

Choose something from the book you'd like to plan into your life.

Write it down here in BIG letters so you don't forget it.

_____

There's just a small space because it needs to be just one thing.

Make sure it's something you want to work on. Something that will make a difference. And something you can change without too many steps. If it's something big you may need to break the final goal down into smaller pieces. Remember the Climbing wall (Step 6).

Now Complete the Planner sheet on the next two pages to build on what you've learned.

Planner Sheet

Make a Plan!

1. What am I going to do?

Just one small thing

2. When am I going to do it?

That way you'll know if you don't do it

3. What problems or difficulties could arise, and how can I overcome them?

4. Is my planned task -

	Yes	No
Useful for understanding or changing how I am?	☐	☐
Specific, so that I will know when I have done it?	☐	☐
Realistic, practical and achievable?	☐	☐

My notes:

MORE THINGS THAT WILL HELP YOU HELP YOURSELF

This little book is a companion to all the ones on the right – it tells you how to get the most from each one.

You can get added help and support by working through the free linked online modules at www.llttf.com. It's an award-winning course, and the number one site for low mood and anxiety recommended by NHS Trusts and teams in England.*

When you've finished working on your current problem, you might want to choose another little book and work on something else in your life. If so, don't forget you'll need this one as well, so hang on to it!

*Bennion et al, 2017. BMJ Open http://bmjopen.bmj.com/content/7/1/e014844